January 3, 1997

Dear Dad,
Wish you all the best for
your birthday and enjoy
looking at our part of
the world!!!
Love,
Shiloh & Ben
Always xo

DISCOVER
WESTERN AUSTRALIA

DISCOVER
WESTERN AUSTRALIA

Jocelyn Burt

UNIVERSITY OF WESTERN AUSTRALIA PRESS

ACKNOWLEDGEMENTS

For their assistance with this book I would like to thank the following: Bruce Ellison and Pat Martin of The Bush Camp, near Kununurra; Stephen Sharpe of Lake Argyle Cruises, Argyle Village; Ian and Sue Sinnamon, Home Valley Station, East Kimberley; Jack and Neroli Roberts, Kununurra; Slingsby Helicopters, Kununurra; Russell Guest 4x4 Safaris, Melbourne; Neil McLeod of Ningaloo Safari Tours, Exmouth; Department of Conservation and Land Management, Western Australia.

PHOTOGRAPHIC NOTES

All the photographs featured as panoramic spreads were taken with a Fuji G617 panoramic camera; most of the other photographs were taken with a Mamiya RB67 camera.

Nearly all the photographs for this book were taken on Fuji RDP film. All the films were processed by Bond Colour Labs, Richmond, Victoria, and I would like to thank Lothar Huber, Merilyn Newnham, Joan Stafford, Peter Knight, Doug Porter and Mark Thomson for excellent service.

FRONT COVER: *Karri forest near Pemberton*
BACK COVER: *Moonrise, Gibson Desert*
OPPOSITE TITLE PAGE: *Bungle Bungle Range*

First published in 1993 by
University of Western Australia Press,
Nedlands, Western Australia, 6009.

National Library of Australia
Cataloguing-in-Publication entry:

Burt, Jocelyn.
    Discover Western Australia

    ISBN 1 875560 21 1.

    1. Western Australia – Guidebooks. I. Title.

919.410463

Consultant Editor H. K. Bradbury
Designed by Susan Eve Ellvey of Designpoint, Perth
Typeset in 12pt Berkeley Book by Lasertype, Perth
Printed by Scott Four Colour Print, Perth

Contents

AN ESSENTIAL AND PRECIOUS FREEDOM

Western Australia is huge. So big are the distances and so far are the horizons that it is said that the locals have a 'thousand yard stare'. Space seems to dominate nearly every visual aspect of the state.

The size of India and half that of Europe, Western Australia totals one third of the continent of Australia. It lies in isolation, separated from eastern Australia by deserts: the nearest interstate city to its capital, Perth, is Adelaide over 2700 kilometres away. In dramatic contrast to its size is its population: in an area covering more than 2.5 million square kilometres, around 90 per cent of the 1.5 million inhabitants (less than one-tenth of Australia's total population) live in the south-western portion between Geraldton, Kalgoorlie and Esperance. Perth has just over one million people.

You must drive through the West to grasp fully this vastness. Fortunately motoring is a delight here as all the major roads are now sealed, and unlike the busy main highways and roads in eastern Australia, there is little traffic. Indeed, it is a joy to explore Western Australia beyond the urban areas, where the population is scattered. Perhaps the wide, white sandy beaches that stretch for many kilometres and are never overcrowded best epitomise the essential and precious freedom offered by the West.

Many of the landscapes of Western Australia are like no other in the country—or anywhere else, for that matter. Its great outback has some of the wildest places on earth, and parts are still 'last frontiers'. Scenically, the West is a land of stunning contrasts. Tall forests give way to granite that studs both mountain range and coastline. The deserts feature red sand dunes, groves of desert oaks, shimmering white salt lakes, and vast stony plains. Some of the most spectacular scenes lie to the north where rugged, colourful ranges are slashed by impressive gorges; lush waterholes beckon weary travellers; and great rivers flow suddenly for a few months of the year. The state has many national parks that protect the natural environment.

In stark contrast to the immensity of Western Australian landscapes is the extraordinary diversity of its ground-level life. The unusual fauna and unique flora attract scientists from all over the world. Some of the marsupials are found only in the West (including the numbat and the quokka), and the waters teem with sea life. But it is the abundance of plants that is astonishing. About half of the continent's total number of approximately 15,000 plant species are found in Western Australia, with more than half that number again being endemic to this state. A wonderful example of the intricacy of nature here is found in the Stirling Range: various species of mountain bells (*Pimelea* species) have developed the art of mimicry to a tee. The shape of birds and insects are mimicked by those flowers that require them for pollination. In a normal year, the best time to see the wildflowers in the southern regions is from mid-September through to early November; in the north, August to September. The rich floral area of Kalbarri, and the inland areas west of Geraldton are usually at their best in September.

The first people to occupy the land were the Australian Aborigines, who came from southern Asia possibly around 40,000 years ago. As in other areas of Australia, they left a legacy of distinctive rock art throughout the state. However, considerable mystery surrounds the Wandjina paintings that are found throughout the Kimberley region. Although for generations in ritual the Aborigines have touched up these strange mouthless figures wearing haloes, they were not the original artists. Local legends say the Wandjinas were Dreamtime supermen who came from the north and west, and on their death they assumed the form of rock paintings.

The earliest confirmed landing by Europeans on Australian soil was in 1616 by the Dutch mariner, Dirk Hartog, at Shark Bay in Western Australia. Later, in 1644, Abel Tasman named the entire continent New Holland. However, it wasn't until the nineteenth century that permanent settlement took place in Western Australia. In 1826, Major Edmund Lockyer led a party of British soldiers and convicts to Albany on the south coast to prevent a French settlement, as the French were exploring the area. Thirty months later another group of British immigrants arrived at the Swan River under the leadership of Captain James Stirling to start the settlement that would eventually become Perth. Although convicts were brought in some years later to overcome labour shortages, unlike most other early Australian cities, Perth was colonised by free settlers, not convicts.

The West is unable to support a large population because much of the terrain is not suitable for high-density living. The state has generated its wealth over the years through the primary industries of wheat, sheep and cattle, and by its minerals. Here are located some of the world's richest mineral deposits, and so important is the contribution of mining to the economy that entire towns have been built to cater for miners—for example, Newman and Tom Price in the Pilbara.

The first payable gold was discovered in the Kimberley in 1885, and a decade later the great reefs in the Coolgardie-Kalgoorlie areas were being mined—and continue to be today. In the 1960s a new mineral boom occurred, with the discoveries of bauxite, oil, nickel, and iron ore. Deposits of iron ore in the Pilbara are some of the largest in the world. Then in the 1970s diamonds were found in the East Kimberley region, and the Argyle Diamond Mine is now the world's biggest producer of rough diamonds, accounting for a third of total world production. Workers commute daily by plane from Kununurra to the mine, situated 100 kilometres by air to the south. One can't help wondering what other treasures lie hidden, waiting to be revealed, in this stupendous, largely untamed land.

With one end in the tropics and the other in a cool temperate zone, Western Australia has some strikingly different climatic conditions that give each region its distinctive characteristics, and challenge the traveller into new awarenesses.

In this book I would like to give readers, and prospective travellers, a taste of what there is to savour of Western Australia, in the hope that they will be inspired to discover its uniqueness and grandeur for themselves. I would also like to share a few of my experiences, which may help fellow travellers plan trips that will maximise enjoyment.

Porongurup Range

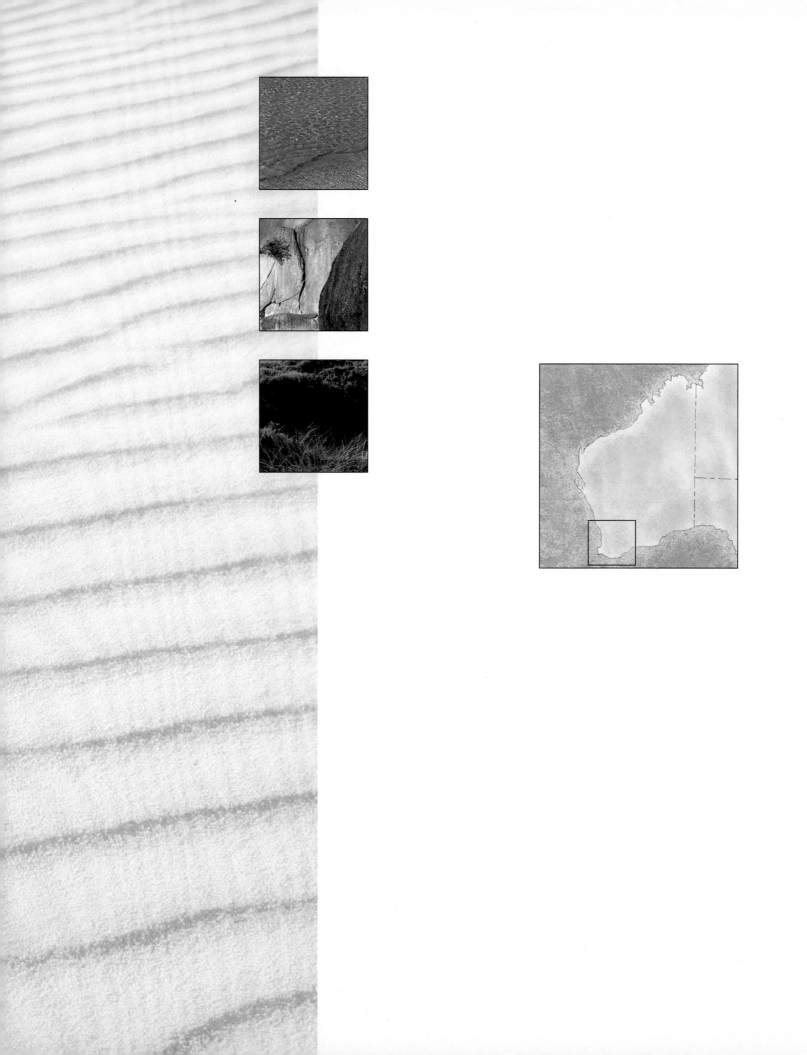

South-West

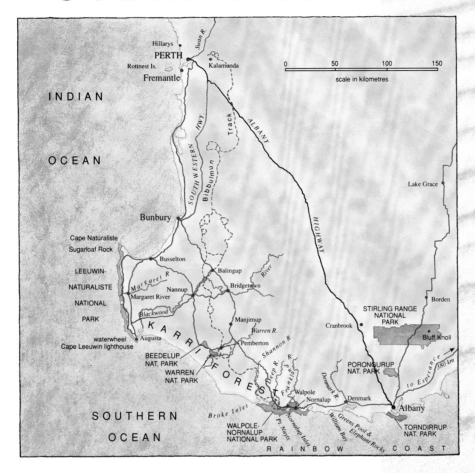

Lying in the lowest corner of the state, the South-West region has an ideal climate for modern life, and for this reason is the most populated. It is cool and wet from May to October and the soils are fertile to support a range of farming. Although the districts around Perth can be warm in summer, the deep south offers a temperate climate favouring fruit growing and dairying. Access to the region is afforded by train, car, bicycle, boat or foot. Bush walking through the jarrah and karri forests is a favourite pursuit. The well-used Bibbulmun track stretches from Kalamunda outside Perth 650 kilometres south to Walpole and offers walkers some spectacular scenery. The South-West is a world of green abundance: towering forests, rich pasture land, rolling vineyards, rushing streams.

PERTH AND FREMANTLE

The Western Australian capital, Perth, is enviably located around the banks of the Swan River which broadens into the tidal Perth Water before reaching the ocean. After a great struggle to survive the initial founding of the colony in 1829, and despite its isolation from the east, Perth has grown into a beautiful and thriving city. It is now becoming one of the commercial centres of the South-East Asia region.

Tree-lined streets, uncluttered suburbs, over 1000 square kilometres of parks, gardens and reserves, and the ideal playground of the Swan River (boat ownership is high here) make Perth a very pleasant home. Without heavy industry in proximity, the city has minimum pollution. Its climate has been described as moderate and even 'idyllically Mediterranean', with mild winters averaging a maximum of 17.6°C. Although the average maximum in summer is 30.3°C, with the city experiencing some very hot days, a sea breeze affectionately known as 'the Fremantle Doctor' eases the heat in the afternoons. And so it is hardly surprising that, with its comfortable blend of urban sophistication, a notably relaxed atmosphere, friendly and hospitable people, clean and enticing beaches washed by the Indian Ocean's surf, Perth has become a firm favourite with many Australian and overseas visitors.

Fremantle, renowned for its historic buildings, and fine marina and yachting complex, is situated only 19 kilometres south of Perth's city centre and is the state's chief port. During the summer of 1986–87, together with Perth, Fremantle hosted the crews of the America's Cup challenges. Thousands of visitors flocked to the event that some consider put Perth 'on the map'.

Perth's most valuable asset is Kings Park, where 162 hectares of natural bushland have been established as a reserve. Set on a hill overlooking the water and the inner city, Kings Park is only a few minutes drive (traffic permitting) from the central business district. Good roads meander though the park and give magnificent views over the city—views that when seen in the afternoon sun, I believe rival Sydney Harbour's grandeur. The more formal gardens at the park's entrance soon give way to natural bushland that in spring is thick with kangaroo paws and other native wildflowers. Take a walk on one of the many paths in the bushland, and you will find it hard to believe that you are in the heart of a big city.

Perth viewed from Kings Park.

ROTTNEST ISLAND

Believed to have been separated from the mainland only around 7000 years ago, this small island lies 20 kilometres off the coast of Fremantle. Ferries ply frequently from Perth, Fremantle and Hillarys, or flights are regularly available. It is such a popular holiday spot with West Australians that bookings for some vacation periods are made on a ballot system; visitors from elsewhere usually see it only on a day trip.

First visited by Dutch mariners in 1658, it was named 38 years later by another Dutch explorer, Willem de Vlamingh, who mistook the island's native quokkas (small bounding marsupials) for giant rats and gave it the Dutch name Rottnest—meaning 'rats nest'. Today, the endearing little quokkas are a major drawcard and are seen at various places around the island.

Rottnest has had an eventful history. In 1839 a penal colony for Aborigines was established here, then during the First World War an internment camp held Austrian and German dissidents. Some of the oldest buildings in Western Australia still stand on the island, and the historic lighthouse once had a ghost. Over the years many ships have been wrecked in its waters, and a Wreck Trail that visitors can follow now marks the graves of many vessels.

History aside, much of the island's charm lies in its coastline, which is indented with attractive bays and inlets, many of them sheltered by extensive reefs. These reefs are easily visible in the clear water, and their intricate lacy patterns help to give Rottnest its special fascination and character. To swim in the rocky pools is a delightful experience—and has been described as like floating in champagne. It is not surprising to learn that these delectable waters support an unusually rich variety of both temperate and tropical plants and animals. This is partly due to the Leeuwin current, a warm ocean current that flows southward down the Western Australian coastline in autumn and winter bringing tropical life to the cooler temperate waters off Perth. As a result, brightly-coloured fish and corals provide a visual feast to divers and snorkellers.

As the use of vehicles is prohibited (except by the authorities), and the relatively flat island is only 11 kilometres long and about four kilometres wide, it is ideal for cycling—and that is the way many visitors explore Rottnest. Indeed, people are encouraged to bring their own bikes. If you prefer to hire one, there are plenty available.

ABOVE: *Rottnest Island*   BELOW: *Quokka*

MARGARET RIVER

The small town of Margaret River lies by the river with the same name, about three-and-a-half hours drive south of Perth and only 10 kilometres from the coast. The town provides a wide choice of accommodation for the tourist keen on the good things in life. In the 1960s viticulture began in the district, and it wasn't long before some exceptionally good wines were being produced. As fine wine goes with good food, it's not surprising that Margaret River is now famous for its eating places, too. Adding even more interest to the area are the many artists, craftspeople and sculptors who now live here. The open air Leeuwin Estate concerts are held each year and feature the best in international performers—Shirley Bassey, Count Basie, The London Philharmonic Orchestra are just some of the illustrious visitors to this little pocket of paradise.

One tourist brochure describes Margaret River as 'a sleepy little town'. My observation was that it is anything but that. On mid-week afternoons in spring when sleepy little towns are snoozing, Margaret River is bustling with people. As you stroll up the main street with all its restaurants, cafes and tearooms, it is easy enough to be tempted by the local fare. Try it, it's good.

However, it is not only the district's gourmet delights and cultural activities that attract people, there is another drawcard: the nearby coast. Part of the Leeuwin-Naturaliste National Park, the beach by the mouth of the Margaret River provides excellent surf for board-riding enthusiasts, and every March or April the important 'Margaret River Masters' surfing competition—part of the international circuit—is held here. As well, there is some lovely scenery at the river mouth, where the sandbar at its entrance gives another dimension of beauty to the river. In summer the sandbar blocks the mouth, resulting in the river waters spreading out to form a lake; in winter the river usually flows freely to the ocean.

In contrast to the surface countryside with its undulating karri and jarrah-studded hills, there is an extensive system of limestone caves in the national park—well over 360 in all. The Mammoth, Lake, Jewel and Moondyne Adventure caves are open to the public. The Mammoth Cave has large caverns, and fossil remains are clearly visible, while the Lake Cave has a stream flowing through it that creates a spectacular underground lake. The Moondyne Adventure and Jewel caves lie near Augusta; the Jewel Cave features some of the longest straw stalactites in the world.

The mouth of the Margaret River

AUGUSTA-CAPE LEEUWIN

On a windswept headland of craggy granite that juts into the sea where the Indian and Southern Oceans meet, stands the old stone Cape Leeuwin lighthouse. Built in 1895, this historic beacon lies nine kilometres from the small coastal town of Augusta, 320 kilometres from Perth.

The coast surrounding the lighthouse grounds is the southernmost part of the Leeuwin-Naturaliste National Park. An important feature of the park is the Leeuwin-Naturaliste Ridge, a belt of limestone and sands overlying granite. Mildly acidic groundwater has worn the limestone to form the many caves for which the area is well-known. The park features spacious beaches, dunes, rocky headlands and high cliffs that give way to vegetation ranging from low scrub heaths to majestic karri forests, all rich with bird life. Near Cape Naturaliste to the north, the craggy granite Sugarloaf Rock is the southernmost breeding ground of the red-tailed tropic bird.

Although the lighthouse is a popular place to visit, there is one intriguing sight nearby that should not be missed: the old waterwheel. Fed by a natural spring in the hill behind, the waterwheel was erected during the same year as the lighthouse to supply water to the keepers' cottages; the large wheel drove a pump that operated until 1928. The calcium-enriched water that continues to flow over the wooden wheel and its channel is slowly turning them both to stone.

Augusta services the national park and provides summer holiday-makers with a variety of accommodation. Keen fishermen are regular visitors, as the town lies by the picturesque mouth of the Blackwood River. However, fishermen are not the only hunters of the river produce: sharks can sometimes be seen gorging on an abundant supply of river and ocean species as the Blackwood swirls into the Southern Ocean. Often in the late afternoon, there is some delightful entertainment provided by pelicans that gather at various spots at the river mouth, waiting for fish scraps thrown out by the fishermen at the end of the day's catch. The sight of these stately birds scrambling in the water to snatch the thrown morsels is both impressive and comical: for once the greedy seagulls, always alert for a handout, find that the competition is just too fierce.

ABOVE: *Blackwood River, Augusta*   BELOW L: *Pelicans, Augusta*   BELOW R: *Cape Leeuwin*

WALPOLE-NORNALUP

Walpole-Nornalup National Park is renowned for its wildflowers, its splendid stands of karri, jarrah and red tingles, and the tranquil Nornalup and Broke inlets. Fed by the Deep, Frankland and Shannon rivers respectively, these waterways are favourite destinations for canoeists. As well, the park has some 40 kilometres of coastline edging the Southern Ocean, and features granite headlands, coves, beaches, dunes, heathlands, and wilderness areas such as Point Nuyts, accessible only by foot. Most visitors exploring the South-West will pass through the park, as it lies by the South Coast Highway, between Manjimup and Albany. However, much of the area is accessible only by four-wheel drive vehicle (4WD), horse trail or by the bush walker intent on 'getting away from it all'. The Bibbulmun Walk Track traverses the park and terminates at Walpole.

People come here in summer to escape the heat of Perth and other northern areas. There is a pleasant camping ground at Coalmine Beach, and the park has many walking trails, both in the karri forest and through open coastal terrain. Knoll Drive loops for five kilometres around a karri-covered hilltop overlooking Nornalup Inlet, and gives tantalising glimpses of the water through the trees. From a small secluded picnic ground there is access to the water.

Karri trees are confined to a relatively small area of high rainfall and rich loamy soil between Cape Leeuwin and Albany, extending inland for about 130 kilometres. The karri (*Eucalyptus diversicolor*) is one of the tallest trees in the world, reaching to almost 90 metres—in Australia it is exceeded only by the mountain ash and alpine ash. It is certainly the West's tallest tree. The karri's hard and heavy timber has proved to be exceptionally durable and moderately resistant to termites. The species has supported a timber industry for over 100 years.

Spring is the best time to see the spectacular wildflower display in the park accompanied by a cacophony of bird chorus. Although the flowers are good in September and October the weather often isn't: over the years my visits to the south coast have usually been dogged by rain—this section of the southern seaboard is not called the 'Rainbow Coast' without reason. On the last morning of one visit, I saw for the first time the true beauty of Nornalup Inlet from the water's edge by Knoll Drive's picnic ground. At sunrise the inlet was heavily veiled in mist, which created a beautiful wintry effect as the early morning sunlight tried to pierce the chill gloom of the fog. Gradually the mist lifted to reveal reflections of the surrounding hills that gave an intense depth and beauty to the scene.

Nornalup Inlet

WILLIAM BAY AND DENMARK

William Bay lies just off the South Coast Highway some 70 kilometres west of Albany and 14 kilometres from Denmark. The main beach is studded with great granite boulders, most of them lying in and around the water's edge; some are splashed with orange lichen. There is some good walking here on fine sands that stretch for several kilometres around the boulders. On a day of wild weather when the sun breaks through to light the rocks, the rolling surf and storm clouds above, the beach is superb.

Just near the carpark, at the eastern end of the beach is Green's Pool, a large pool of calm water that provides safe swimming within a natural barrier of rocks. The morning that I photographed the beach at sunrise, I met four elderly ladies who had come for a swim. For the past eight months they had kept this appointment at Green's Pool—even through winter, despite the weather. The exception was during thunderstorms. 'Our husbands don't like us coming down in storms', one lady cheerfully said. Another explained that in bad weather the waves beyond the protecting rocks can get so big that they obliterate the protecting barrier. They swam for about thirty minutes. I did not envy them at all as I knew the water was very cold.

My favourite spot in this national park is Elephant Rocks. Lying about five minutes walk from another carpark near Green's Pool, a delightful beach nestles in a small cove full of elephantine rocks. The sea was calm when I was there, but I imagine that a strong surf rolling between the rocks would be quite a sight.

About two kilometres further on is Madfish Bay. I went down to investigate it because the name sounded intriguing. Here an island of granite gave shelter to a small cove that provided more safe swimming. A notice advised not to disturb the nesting birds, and to watch out for snakes.

The delightful little town of Denmark, set by the river with the same name, is popular with summer visitors who enjoy staying in country-style accommodation and experiencing the unique environment of this timber town where the forest meets the sea. Stroll by the lazy Denmark River, take a paddle boat ride, or picnic on the shady lawns of the river bank. You'll understand why Denmark now is very popular amongst West Australians who desire an unspoilt, tranquil place to live.

ABOVE: *Green's Pool, William Bay*   BELOW: *Elephant Rocks, William Bay*

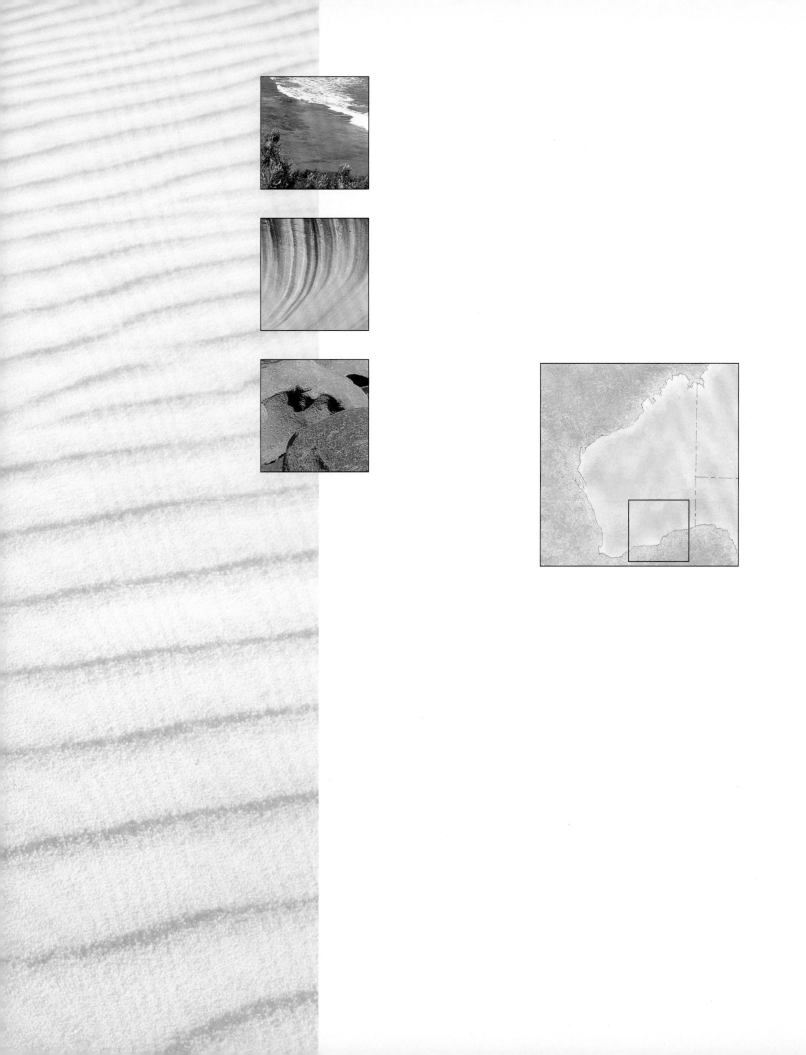

Great Southern and Goldfields

The Great Southern and Goldfields regions are drier than the South-West and, once the coast is left behind for the more arid inland, the summer days become hotter and the winter nights colder. The coastline of the Great Southern is craggy and isolated, often battered by the cold Southern Ocean. We leave the green countryside of the southern seaboard behind and travel north to the historic towns serving the goldfields. Vegetation changes dramatically as sheep and wheat farms give way to open woodland dotted by perfumed sandalwood plants and 'jam' trees (yes, they smell like raspberry jam when burnt on the open fire). Looking around it is hard to believe that this seemingly endless semi-desert hundreds of kilometres from the coast was once home to thousands of goldrush diggers in small towns connected by camel trains.

ALBANY

Situated on the south coast 413 kilometres from Perth, Albany is the oldest settlement in the state, and is now known as the Heart of the Rainbow Coast. The town's rich history is reflected in its old buildings and memorabilia, including the brig *Amity* that brought the first settlers to Western Australia in 1826. The spectacular scenery at Albany together with the excellent accommodation available make this town a leading holiday destination.

The town nestles by the magnificent granite-fringed Princess Royal Harbour in King George Sound. Some of the finest views are from the Princess Royal Fortress—popularly known as 'The Forts'—which stands high on a hill overlooking the harbour and King George Sound. Restored in recent years and now a major tourist attraction, this old fortress was built in 1893, and with one on Thursday Island in north Queensland, was jointly funded by all the Australian states before federation to protect Australia from what was then known as the 'Russian threat'. The great guns are now at rest, quietly pointing over the bay.

There is more history, though somewhat grisly, to relive at Whaleworld, the whaling museum at Frenchman's Bay, 20 kilometres around Princess Royal Harbour from Albany's town centre. Set in the original whaling station, the museum is complete with the restored *Cheynes IV* whale chaser boat. Even before it ceased operating in 1978 the station was a major tourist attraction—though heaven knows why, as the stench was so terrible it defied description, and the slaughter house made you weep for the whales (I had the misfortune of seeing it then as a travelling companion wanted to buy a whale tooth). It is still a moving experience to see the museum's well-presented history of whaling, but now there is peace at the station—with no smells—and it is worth visiting.

Albany's best scenery lies just south of the town in the Torndirrup National Park. Here bleak granite bluffs give way to stone-studded small bays and sandy beaches that even on stormy days, when the air is damp and the wind stirs the seas to crash against the rocks, display a marvellously wild beauty. Dramatic formations such as the Natural Bridge, the Gap and the Blowholes lure many visitors, and there is good fishing from some of the beaches. But this coast is dangerous and many people have lost their lives when king waves—those colossal waves that break quite unexpectedly— have swept over rocks that seem ideal fishing spots.

ABOVE: *Salmon Holes, Torndirrup National Park*   BELOW: *Whaleworld, Frenchman's Bay*

Princess Royal Fortress

STIRLING RANGE

There is a public holiday in September. A bitterly cold wind blows, bringing in ominously grey, moisture-laden clouds that swirl defiantly around the high peaks of the range. By 8.00a.m. the large carpark is half full; by lunch time it will be packed, and cars will string the road that leads to it. Two coach-loads of children arrive to join the throng of people who are already on the walking track, appearing like a line of slow-moving ants as they plod upwards towards the 1109-metre-high summit, three kilometres from the carpark. The well-formed trail is steep and although it is obvious that many walkers are very unfit, they show a cheerful determination to reach the top, even if it takes much longer than the advised time of three-to-four hours for the round trip. These people have come to walk one of Western Australia's most popular hikes: Bluff Knoll, the highest peak in the Stirling Range.

The Stirling Range is situated about 80 kilometres from Albany, and like the Porongurup Range lying to its south, rises abruptly over the district's broad rural plains. It is also a national park that has a resident ranger. However, that is where the similarity between the two ranges ends; indeed, it is surprising to find just how different in character these two places are, given their relatively close proximity. At first glance, some people may find the Stirling Range bleak—even grim—but once they explore the park and see the range against a backdrop of dramatic clouds lit by sunshine, they will fall under its spell.

The national park protects the range's entire system of rugged hills that run in an east-west direction for 55 kilometres. In some places bold bluffs and craggy peaks rise to over 1000 metres; between May and September they may even wear a mantle of snow. Thick scrub covers much of the slopes that give way to rough stony sections near the higher parts. The park also includes some plains, where heaths and woodlands occur; in spring they, and the lower mountain slopes, become a paradise for botanists. The abruptness and drama of the landforms of the Stirling Range has led to the evolution—in typical Western Australian style—of plants occurring nowhere else in the world. For visitors interested in botany, the town of Cranbrook displays information about the flora of the Stirling Range.

ABOVE: *Stirling Range* BELOW L: *Wildflowers, Stirling Range* BELOW R: *Summit, Bluff Knoll*

WAVE ROCK

Wave Rock, as it is aptly called, lies on the outskirts of Hyden, in the wheat belt of the Great Southern region, 350 kilometres east of Perth. For interstate travellers it is not an easy place to reach as it lies well away from other scenic attractions. However, if you have the time, it is worth seeing. Appearing as a wave frozen in stone, this extraordinary granite formation has been weathered and worn relentlessly by nature over a very long period of time. For people who have only seen it in photographs, it may seem smaller than they had imagined, as the use of wide-angle lenses can sometimes disguise its true size. Stretching for 70 metres, and ribboned with colours from chemical deposits washed out of the rock by rain, it rises to about 15 metres over the rocky floor.

Allow more than a few minutes to explore this unusual feature, for you will then experience the odd sensation that at any moment the rock will actually break, just as a wave breaks in the surf. At Hippo's Yawn, a huge cavernous rock that looks remarkably like the gaping mouth of a hippopotamus lying 15 minutes from Wave Rock, there is a similar strange sensation: if you stand underneath it for too long, there is the distinct feeling the 'jaws' might snap.

Wave Rock has some odd acoustics, too: when a car revs its engine in the nearby caravan park while you are by the wall, it sounds as if the vehicle is somewhere on top of the cliff. When I was last there the caravan park and carpark were full of vehicles coming and going as it was a long-weekend at the start of the school holidays. Children were everywhere, and it wasn't long before they found an ideal playground: Wave Rock's curved wall drew them like a magnet for their ball games. I retreated to the walk on top of the rock to appreciate what Western Australia offers the most of: pure, peaceful space.

Wave Rock

ESPERANCE

Set around Esperance Bay on the south coast some 725 kilometres from Perth, the town of Esperance lies about half-way between Cape Leeuwin and the state border. This may seem to be a long way from the more settled areas of the far south-west corner, but the district has some of the most beautiful coastline in Australia, and it is hardly surprising that the town has become a popular tourist destination. For travellers from eastern Australia, it is a particularly refreshing place to rest after the long drive across the Nullarbor Plain.

First settled in 1893, Esperance was the port for the Coolgardie goldfield; today, it serves the southern part of the West, shipping minerals, salt and wheat. The town is also the base for a very active fishing industry. In 1987 Australia's first wind farm was built at the edge of the town to harness the coast's strong winds for electricity. Standing on a high ridge near Salmon Beach, its six wind turbine generators are linked to the local power grid and save the diesel-run power station a considerable amount of fuel. These modern windmills are easily seen from the Tourist Loop drive.

If visitors have time for only one excursion at Esperance, it ought to be the Tourist Loop drive. For 18 of its 34 kilometres the road hugs the coast, giving splendid views of the many unbelievably white sandy beaches, granite coves and bluffs, and the myriad islands comprising the Archipelago of the Recherche. There are ample carparks that provide walking access to the beaches.

Cape Le Grand National Park, 45 kilometres east of Esperance, provides more spectacular scenery. One notable feature is its massive outcrops of granite. Headlands walled in grey granite drop to the surging swell of the Southern Ocean, and oddly shaped weatherworn rocks litter the coastal slopes and beaches as if carelessly flung down by a giant hand. Like elsewhere along this coast, the dazzling white sands contrast dramatically with a sea that varies in colour from a pale aquamarine in the shallows, graduating through a series of rich blues to a deep navy further out. In places these white sands are so fine they squeak underfoot, and when pressed in the hand feel like talcum powder.

Cape Le Grand

West Beach, Esperance

EUCLA

Of all the settlements by the Eyre Highway that crosses the Nullarbor Plain (meaning in Latin, 'no tree'), Eucla is the most interesting, and historic. Named by Edward John Eyre on his epic journey across the continent in 1841, it lies close to the shores of the Great Australian Bight and only 24 kilometres from the South Australian border; Perth is a far 1432 kilometres away.

In 1877, on a site nearer the coast than Eucla's present day position, a telegraph station was built to provide a direct link between the eastern states and Western Australia; however, in 1920 a new telegraph line was opened along the railway, situated further north, and shortly afterwards the southern line was disconnected. Later the settlement was relocated five kilometres further inland to an 87-metre-high hilltop, where it is today.

The drifting dunes that are a prominent feature of the coast here gradually buried Eucla's buildings; the only one visible today is the ruins of the telegraph station—and it won't be long before that too completely disappears. Originally these great hills of sand were firmly held by vegetation, but by the end of the nineteenth century armies of introduced rabbits had reached the district and in a short time devoured enough of this plant cover to precipitate massive wind erosion. The bare dunes then began to drift.

Eucla's Sahara-like sand hills are magnificent, and best seen when the shadows cast by a low sun give them an unearthly, sculpted appearance. They are now part of a small national park. An unsealed road runs from the settlement to the carpark; from there it is only a few minutes walk to the old telegraph station, and about 45 minutes to the beach and the remains of a jetty that provided the only anchorage for hundreds of kilometres. Few people seem to venture beyond the ruins and the track leading to the beach—but then the elements often do not encourage much exploration. The region is known for its wind, and the dunes are no place to be when the wind is so strong that it lifts the sand to act like sandpaper against bare skin.

ABOVE: *Dunes, Eucla*   BELOW: *Telegraph station ruins*

KALGOORLIE

Lying 597 kilometres east of Perth, Kalgoorlie is the hub of the West's south-eastern mining region. Its famed Golden Mile is one of the world's richest reefs of gold, and the nearby town of Boulder—nowadays a virtual extension of Kalgoorlie—is situated on it.

Gold was first discovered in the district by an Irishman, Paddy Hannan, in 1893, and the inevitable rush followed. The vast open-cut mines of today are a far cry from the first prospectors' diggings. Giant trucks moving back and forth far below in the huge gouged pits resemble small toys when viewed from the top. Only two underground mines, complete with poppet heads that stand close to the town's shopping centre, are still operating. One of these old mines is just under a kilometre deep. 'Underneath your feet are tunnels that spread out in a maze below the town', a shop-assistant informed me.

I liked Kalgoorlie. It had an air of prosperity, and I found it to be the most interesting, and attractive of all Australia's mining towns. Just the fact that gold is mined here somehow adds to the atmosphere; certainly gold has more romance and appeal than nickel, Kalgoorlie's other source of mineral wealth. As well, the town has many historic buildings that have retained their character and charm.

The visitor can choose from a multitude of engaging activities. You can explore an old mine or view an open-cut one; there is an hour-long train journey around the Golden Mile, an emu farm to see, and for gamblers, there is the world's only legal bush two-up school, where pennies are tossed. The School of Mines has a fine collection of minerals and replicas of famous nuggets found in the area, and there is the excellent Museum of the Goldfields, which I was assured was the finest in the West. It certainly lives up to its claim. From the top of the old poppet head that guards the museum's entrance there are good views over the town and mines.

Poppet Head, Museum of the Goldfields, Kalgoorlie

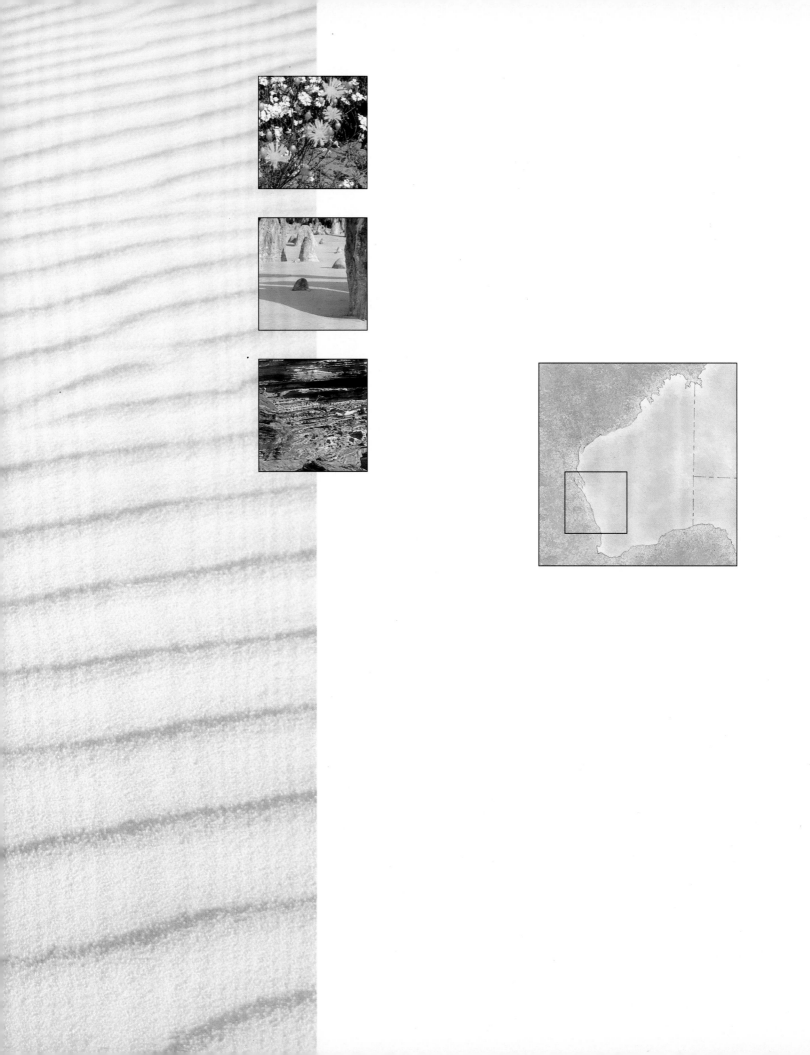

Murchison

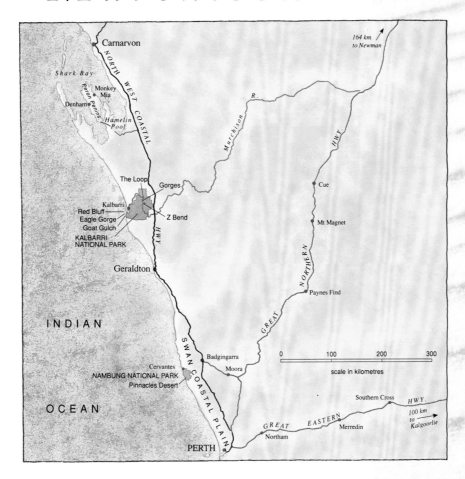

In the central Murchison region coastal weather patterns provide a pleasant climate, but inland it can be very warm in summer. The moderate conditions of the south give way to a hot Mediterranean climate that still retains the winter months as its wettest. Small farm holdings get larger as the soils become less fertile and in these regions the well-known Australian sheep and cattle stations commence, signalling the lifestyle of the pioneer who is never out of mind in these 'frontier' lands. The fishing is superb in this area and the wildflowers excel, the paper-like everlastings carpeting the terrain from Moora through to Cue and Carnarvon during spring.

WILDFLOWERS

The abundance of flora in this state is thought to have occurred because the huge south-west plate of Australia is geologically one of the most undisturbed landmasses on the Earth's surface. It was isolated millions of years ago by sea on one side and desert on the other. As a result there developed the remarkably specialised flora found here today.

So it is not surprising that the West is known as the Wildflower State—even some of the registration plates on the state's vehicles remind you of that. It is the utter profusion in which the plants bloom that is so wonderful. Natural scrubland and plains are transformed into wild gardens blazing with colour, their floral wealth spilling out to the very edges of the road and filling the air with sweet scents. Even in the rural areas, every vestige of land that has escaped being cultivated is likely to display a mass of flowers. In just a few square metres an astonishing variety of plants can be found, and many flowers seem more vibrant and diverse in form than those in the eastern states. Some of the strangest are the kangaroo paws—one species, *Anigozanthos manglesii*, is Western Australia's floral emblem.

Perhaps the richness of the West's flora is best illustrated by its banksias: by the 1980s there were 58 named species, of which 46 were found in Western Australia. Only one of these was also native to two other Australian states, and most of the other 45 were confined to very small areas of Western Australia. The remaining twelve species originated in the eastern half of the continent.

Some of the best places to see flowers are near Badgingarra and Kalbarri in the Murchison area, Stirling Range, the Lake Grace district, and around Fitzgerald River. In a year of good winter rains the country between Mount Magnet and Paynes Find, like much of the Murchison, has incredible displays of everlasting daisies, while masses of tiny velleia dust the earth like pink-tinged snow beneath mulga scrub and eucalypt woodlands. During spring many towns stage wildflower exhibitions, and these are always worth seeing.

Every year people—including many scientists—come from all over Australia to observe the flora. There are, for example, more than 300 species of native orchid to see. There are plenty of wildflower tours available—but choose your tour carefully, as there are some that expect you to see the flowers only while hurtling around the country at 100 km/h. Yet others are hosted by tour guides who invite tourists to attempt to count the numbers of species in a square metre. Be prepared to observe more than fifty!

ABOVE: *Spring, Darling Ranges*   BELOW L: *Possum Banksia*   BELOW R: *Kangaroo Paw*

Wildflowers, near Mt Magnet

THE PINNACLES DESERT

It has been likened to ancient ruins, a weird graveyard, lost cities, and a scene from the Middle East. Certainly the Pinnacles Desert is one of the country's strangest landscapes; indeed, it is almost alien to the character of Australia as it has almost no vegetation.

Lying on the Swan Coastal Plain 245 kilometres north of Perth in the Nambung National Park, the Pinnacles Desert features an immense collection of limestone spires that rise from bare golden sand. They developed thousands of years ago under the ground, when the climate here was much wetter. Eventually, erosion gradually exposed the hardened limestone shapes that range from the size of a man's hand to four metres in height. It is thought that what we see is merely the tip of each pinnacle that extends deep below ground level.

Access to the Pinnacles is through the fishing village of Cervantes, situated near the national park. Once in the desert, motorists follow the marked one-way track that loops for about four kilometres through the spires. As there are numerous parking bays along the way, it is possible to stop for photographs—which is just as well, as the place is a photographers' paradise. The best time of day for photography is at sunset, when the spires turn a rich gold in the sun's low light; if there are clouds, the scenes are stunning. I find that the morning's first sunlight is not as good as late afternoon—in the morning the sun has to climb over a hill to light the spires.

As well as the photo opportunities afforded by the early mornings and late afternoons, it is at the extremities of the day when that wonderful sense of wilderness comes easily in the Pinnacles Desert. However, the sense can be elusive, even here, should you be sharing the experience with a large number of people. Up until 1986 the Pinnacles Desert was a veritable wilderness as access was difficult. The last section of the road then was a 'horror stretch' and so studded with stones that driving over it was like navigating a boat through a dangerous coral reef. Today, the Pinnacles loop is an easy drive on sand, approached by a good gravel road, and has become a 'must' for visitors to Western Australia.

Pinnacles Desert

KALBARRI

Lying 590 kilometres north of Perth, the town of Kalbarri with its pleasant climate, good fishing and safe waters for swimming and boating, is more than just a seaside holiday resort. It is the gateway to a major national park; as well, the district is renowned for its amazing variety of spring wildflowers.

Kalbarri National Park virtually surrounds the township. One of the grandest scenes of the coast is from Red Bluff, only a few kilometres south of the town, where high cliffs indented with weathered, multicoloured gullies drop to the Indian Ocean. The names of these gullies are equally colourful: Rainbow Valley, Pot Alley Gorge, Goat Gulch, Eagle Gorge, Shell House, Layer Cake Gorge and Madman's Rock. Another wonderful sight is the long wall of cliffs at Castle Cove; at sunset it turns a soft gold just before the sun slips below the horizon. From the carpark, 16 kilometres from Kalbarri, it is only a few minutes walk to these cliffs and the Natural Bridge, just beyond. There is also some good walking along a marked trail that meanders over the clifftops.

Beyond the town to the east the national park has some very different scenery. Here the Murchison River cuts its way through sandstone for about 80 kilometres before spilling into its wide estuary by the town. Good firm sandy roads lead to various vantage points where visitors can view the Murchison Gorge; better still is the scenery in the park viewed from a walk along the clifftop at The Loop.

Most people take the five-minute walk at The Loop to Nature's Window, a large weathered arch of rock that frames the panorama of the gorge and river as it loops back on itself. There are even better views further along at the 'Z' Bend and there are information bays, barbecue facilities and public conveniences in the vicinity. After the first gully is crossed, however, the terrain becomes extremely rough and no more cairns mark the way. From here on the walking is hard.

ABOVE: *Murchison River Gorge*　BELOW L: *Kalbarri*　BELOW R: *Wildflowers, Kalbarri*

SHARK BAY

Lying south of Carnarvon, Shark Bay is a large shallow inlet divided into two arms by the Peron Peninsula, one of the distinctive western landforms of Australia. True to its name, the inlet is home for plenty of sharks. On the western side of the peninsula is Shark Bay's principal town, Denham, which is linked by a good bitumen road to the North West Coastal Highway, 130 kilometres away. From Denham, the bitumen continues for another 25 kilometres to a small settlement, Monkey Mia. It is to Monkey Mia that people come to see the dolphins.

These are no captive dolphins, but wild ones who choose to come close to the shore to communicate with humans; indeed, some appear to delight in attracting attention. Nowhere else in the world does this phenomenon occur. Since about 1964 bottlenose dolphins have been coming in for handouts of fish and they have established relationships with the local population. However, it wasn't until the road was sealed in the 1980s that tens of thousands of visitors started pouring in to see these social creatures. Today, rangers strictly control the feeding and the amount of human contact given the dolphins by visitors. Rangers keep a constant lookout for stress to the animals. It appears that the dolphins are coping more easily with the crowds nowadays than in the earlier years.

Of the 40 dolphins that visit the shores of Monkey Mia, seven generally come in daily. When I was there, only three came in during the morning. Watching these lovable creatures playfully rolling around us as we stood in the water, I was surprised at just how easily they captured my heart.

Shark Bay has another unique feature: the stromatolites, lying in Hamelin Pool at the south-eastern end of the bay. Stromatolites are the most ancient life form known on Earth, and the ones here are the most abundant and diverse in the world. Resembling some kind of fossilised unopened toadstools, these living structures are formed by blue-green algae trapping sediment that gradually builds into distinctive club-shaped columns growing up to half a metre. The best time to see them is at low tide, when they are exposed.

ABOVE: *Stromatolites*   BELOW: *A familiar scene at Monkey Mia*

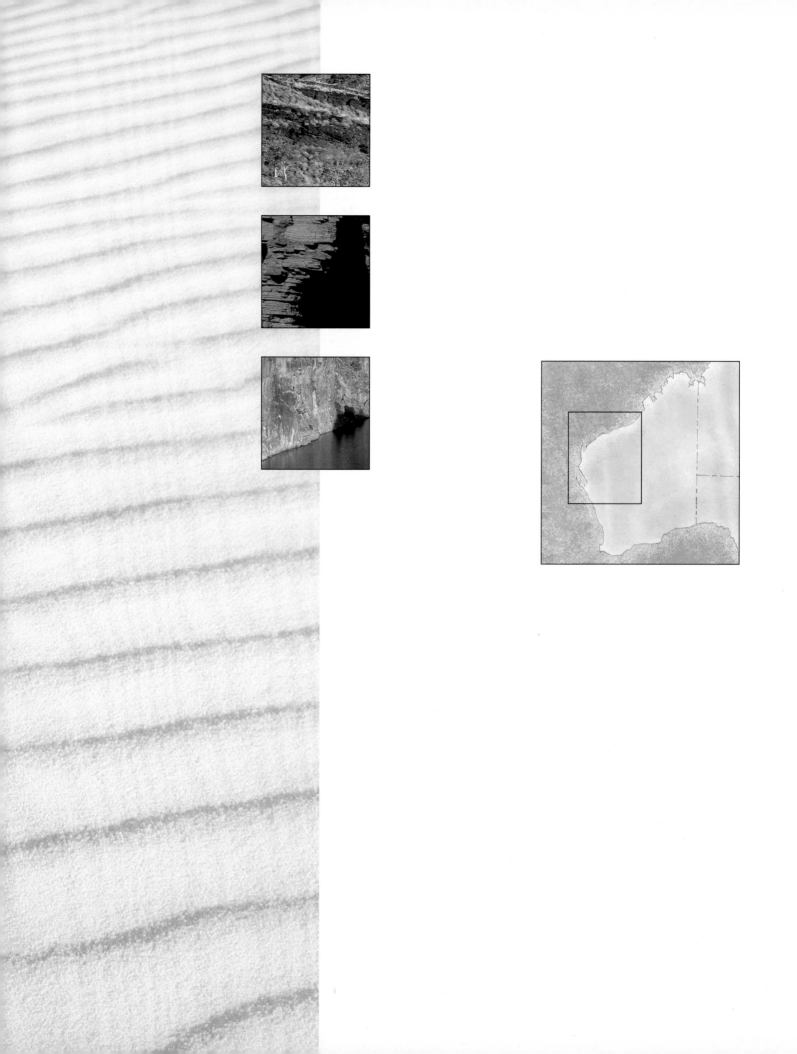

Pilbara

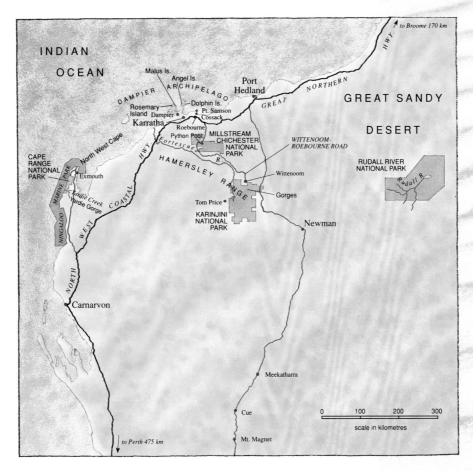

As one moves further north towards the tropics, temperatures increase and the four seasons become two: the wet and the dry. The Pilbara region stretches inland from the coast between Roebourne and Port Hedland in the north-west of the state to the eastern edge of the Great Sandy Desert. Little rain falls here, and in summer the temperatures soar to around 49°C. Winter temperatures are in the twenties, with cold nights inland—in July it is not uncommon for the nights to drop to 0°C in some areas. Much of the Pilbara is ironstone country and it is here the iron-ore-rich mines lie. Part of Australia's outback, this region is renowned for its harsh, stony ranges and gorges that are extraordinarily colourful.

CAPE RANGE

For travellers not familiar with the region, Cape Range comes as a pleasant surprise after travelling the 225 kilometres to Exmouth on North West Cape—the small peninsula that juts into the Indian Ocean north of Carnarvon. The rugged, barren-looking range is a massive fold of limestone slashed with deep canyons and gorges tinted with a variety of warm earthy colours. To the west, its slopes give way to more than 50 kilometres of pristine-white sandy beaches that offer solitude as well as beauty. Both the range and the beaches are part of the Cape Range National Park; immediately offshore on the western side is the Ningaloo Marine Park, which protects a superb coral reef—the longest west coast tropical reef in the world—lying in water renowned for its clarity.

The canyons on the eastern side are unlike any others I have seen in Australia. Two roads suitable for two-wheel-drive (2WD) vehicles give access from the Exmouth road: the Shothole Canyon Road winds for about 12 kilometres along the floor of a deep gorge, while the Charles Knife Road runs steeply for about 15 kilometres over a razor-like ridge before ending at a capped oil well. On both sides of this road colourful chasms dramatically yawn open, showing a classic example of massive erosion that has occurred over the ages.

As the unmarked track over the range to the coast was for 4WD vehicles only, and required local knowledge as to how to find the way, I decided to take a day tour from Exmouth. After getting an excellent overview of the whole area, I did my own exploring and made a beeline for Yardie Gorge, on the western side of the range. Here, craggy rust-coloured cliffs line a permanent waterhole in Yardie Creek; a sandbar blocks its entrance to the sea when the creek is not in flood. Black-banded wallabies live on the lower slopes of the gorge, and there is plenty of birdlife.

There was easy access to Yardie Gorge via the good coastal road from Exmouth, and I used the camping ground near the entrance of the gorge as my base. By far the best walking, both for good scenic views and for negotiating the terrain, was on the southern side of the gorge early in the morning; the northern side was dangerously rough. I recommend that the visitor wears hiking boots as any type of canvas shoes are unsuitable footwear in this terrain.

Yardie Gorge, Cape Range

DAMPIER ARCHIPELAGO

Named after the English buccaneer William Dampier who first visited the area in 1688, the Dampier Archipelago lies within about a 60 kilometre radius off Dampier in the Pilbara. Of the 42 rocky islands in the group, 25 are nature reserves supporting a wide variety of flora and fauna—there is a huge number of birds here. The archipelago is also an offshore playground for the community in the nearby town of Dampier.

In recent years commercial boat trips to some of the islands have been established. Fishing is the main tourist attraction and there are some good deep sea and reef fishing tours. I was fortunate to be shown the archipelago by friends living in Dampier. We left at sunrise. Our boat skimmed over the dark blue sea towards low-lying islands covered in rust-coloured rocks that glowed warmly in the early morning sunlight. The first stop was the Malus Islands, a group of four isles linked by sand spits. Here, a whaling station commenced operations in 1870, and when it closed down three years later two large pots used for boiling down the blubber were left behind. We found them set back from the beach in a cove, rusted by the elements, nestling among some flowering mulla mullas.

At Rosemary Island, Sturt desert pea scrambled over the white sands of the beach that curved around the small bay. This place is noted for its rock wallabies, elusive on this occasion. Angel Island was memorable for its rock formations: grey pillars of stone gave way to clusters of jagged rusty tors that reared by dunes behind the beach that, with some difficulty, we had managed to reach. It is not easy navigating in these waters as there are many treacherous reefs—and not all have been charted. There are strange tides, too. That day on Angel Island, the tide was coming in, with a very strong pull; yet according to the timetable for Dampier, not far away, the tide was going out.

In Flying Foam Passage, lying between Angel Island and Dolphin Island—the largest in the archipelago—a big school of dolphins had a grand time playing with our boat: repeatedly they crossed the bow staying very close to us, and as they leapt out of the water we could hear great 'whooshes' of air being expelled. It was a thrilling sight.

ABOVE: *Angel Island, Dampier Archipelago*   BELOW: *Whalers' pots*

HAMERSLEY RANGE

With a length of nearly 400 kilometres and a maximum width of 150 kilometres, the vast Hamersley Range is a significant feature of the Pilbara region. It is also the source of much of Australia's iron-ore wealth, and there are a number of mines in the area. Most of the Hamersley Range is protected in the Karijini National Park, formerly the Hamersley Range National Park, renamed and now jointly managed by its traditional Aboriginal owners.

Karijini is the West's second biggest national park after Rudall River, and draws many visitors each winter; summers can be unbearably hot. Its main attractions are the spectacular gorges fissuring the plateau that tops this part of the range. From the small settlement of Wittenoom lying at the base of the range, roads lead up to the plateau, the park's camping grounds, and to the gorges.

Walking paths to good vantage points reveal steeply terraced walls of chocolate, red and rusty browns; these vivid colours are accentuated by the white trunks of snappy gums and lush vegetation beside pools of water lying deep below. Probably the most spine-chilling sight is the view over Knox and Red gorges, where perpendicular walls plunge approximately 150 metres. Fortunately, guard rails have now been erected at the lookout.

Less threatening and more intimate than these gorges is my favourite gorge, Kalamina. With its craggy chocolate-coloured walls, shaded pools and sweetly scented vegetation, it is the quintessence of all Karajini's gorges. Access is easy, and there is some relaxed walking through the gorge to Rock Arch Pool, about a half-hour walk from the main pool and waterfalls below the carpark.

There is one gorge not in the national park that, in my view, is one of the most colourful in Australia: Wittenoom Gorge, lying just beyond the town of Wittenoom. I never cease to marvel at its brilliant variety of colours, especially in spring, when a profusion of wildflowers splash even more vibrant hues across its face. From Wittenoom a bitumen road runs for 11 kilometres to the old asbestos mine site. Walking here can be a rather eerie experience, as abandoned machinery dots the landscape, and you can see the holes in the rock face where men mined for blue asbestos. About ten people live in the gorge.

Kalamina Gorge, Hamersley Range

Wittenoom Gorge

MILLSTREAM AND THE CHICHESTER RANGE

Less than an hour's drive from each other in the West Pilbara, two very different places form the Millstream-Chichester National Park, lying off the Wittenoom-Roebourne road. Millstream's beautiful lily-covered pool has long been a drawcard for visitors seeking a refreshing antidote from the Pilbara's heat and dust. Shaded by paperbarks and palms (including the unique Millstream palm), the pool wells from a natural spring and flows into the Fortescue River. The lilies and water ferns were planted many years ago when the land was a sheep station; the old homestead still stands near the main lily pond. There is more precious shade along the nearby Fortescue River, providing some idyllic camp sites.

During my first visit to Millstream in the 1970s it was under threat by a proposed dam that would have flooded the area, and all visitors were asked to sign a petition against it. Fortunately, the plan was dropped and in the early 1980s Millstream was included in a national park. Since then there has been a considerable amount of care given it by the park's staff. However, on my last visit I was saddened to see that a severe fire had swept through, leaving many paperbarks and palms badly charred. It had been started by a panicky tourist suffering from heat exhaustion who, thinking himself to be lost, had lit a fire to attract attention to his plight. 'He wasn't all that far away from the homestead, after all', said the ranger, who assured me that given a few good wet seasons the vegetation would recover.

In contrast, the Chichester Range is a sparsely vegetated arid region of rolling hills so littered with rocks that in places it looks as if a giant tip truck has been at work. I call this 'painted desert' country, because warmly-coloured rust, pink, and chocolate-hued rocks jostle for room among domes of golden spinifex and white-barked snappy gums. I always like to spend a night at Python Pool at the foot of the range, as at sunrise the high rocky walls around the pool blaze briefly, spilling fiery colours over the water. I've never come across any pythons here, but apparently they often used to be seen lying in the pool's cool water in the bygone days when camel teams passed through.

ABOVE: *Millstream*   BELOW: *Chichester Range*

COSSACK

One of Western Australia's most historic towns, Cossack lies on the coast just south of Point Samson and 13 kilometres from Roebourne in the Pilbara. The first settlers came here in 1863 and named it Tien Tsin after the barque that brought the small group; after bearing various other names including Port Walcott, it was officially named Cossack in 1871.

As the first port in north-western Australia, it became a vital gateway to the Pilbara and played an important role in the development of the region. From here camel teams loaded stores and transported them over the Chichester Range to the inland stations, and then returned to the coast with the woolclip. Cossack was also the base for a large pearling industry that brought many nationalities to the district. However, by the early 1900s the town had ceased to be an important government centre, and gradually over the years the population dwindled so much that by the early 1950s it was virtually a ghost town. Two decades later the National Trust of Australia classified it as a heritage site and during the 1980s a restoration program began.

Today, most of the old stone buildings have been restored, and the town has a cared-for look about it. A permanent caretaker lives in the Police Barracks and provides a limited amount of accommodation for backpackers. The impressive Court House is now a museum, and the equally attractive Post and Telegraph Office is an art gallery; visitors may even find an exhibition in progress. As well as the attractive old buildings, Cossack has some fine scenery. At Reader Head lookout a panoramic view sweeps over the spacious Settlers Beach towards Jarman Island; below the lookout there is access to the beach, which is a good one for walking and swimming.

Court House, Cossack

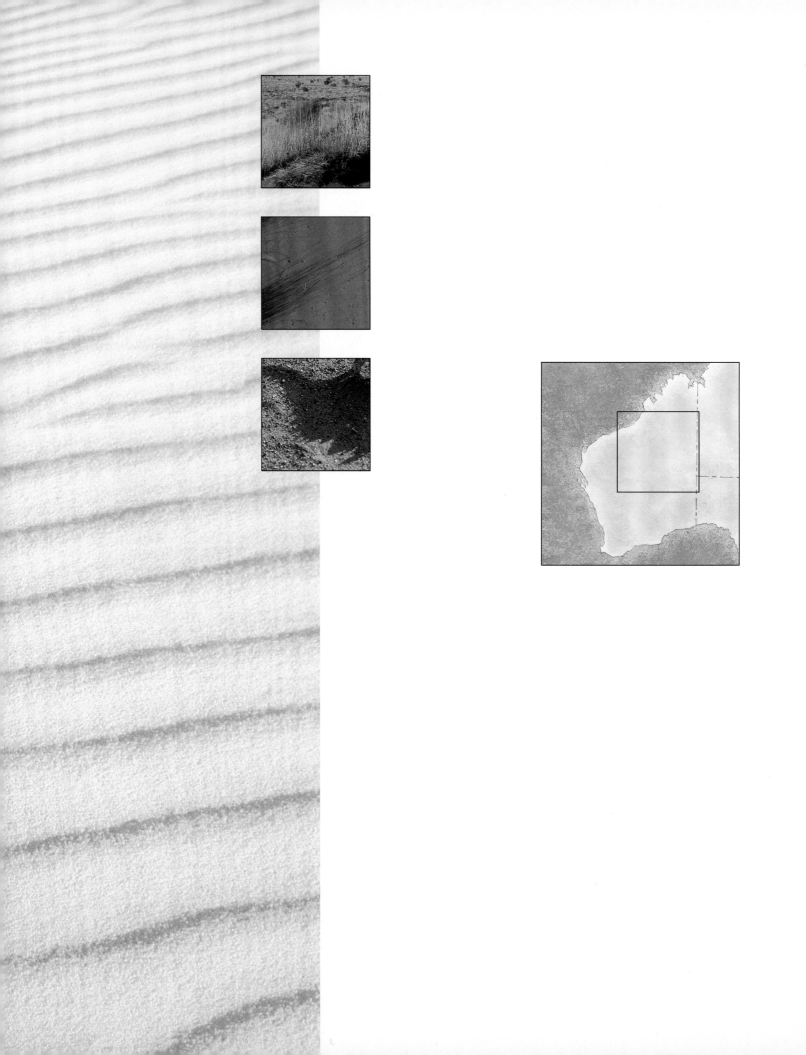

Deserts

Of Australia's six major deserts, three cover a large portion of Western Australia: the Great Sandy, the Gibson, and the Great Victoria deserts. Although the Tanami Desert lies mostly in the Northern Territory, the north-west corner pushes into Western Australia. Winter is the best—and safest—time to visit the desert regions, as the days are warm and the nights cold; the summers are unbearably hot. In normal years, very little rain falls in these remote regions; when rain does fall, it may treble the amount that falls annually. It is after these exceptionally heavy rains that the spring wildflowers transform the usually harsh-looking sandy expanses into veritable gardens.

CANNING STOCK ROUTE

The best way to experience the West's deserts is to travel the Canning Stock Route. The longest stock route in Australia, the Canning runs for more than 1700 kilometres through the Tanami Desert in the north to the Great Sandy and Gibson deserts further south. One of the last great outback adventures for 4WD enthusiasts, it has been described as the world's longest and loneliest drive through one country, with the exception of Siberia, as it passes through no settlements, and there are no fuel stations. Only people who are very well-prepared and have suitable vehicles should undertake this challenging journey during the cooler months of the year.

The route was established by the surveyor Alfred Canning who, between 1907 and 1910, sank 52 wells about 30 kilometres apart between Wiluna in the south and Halls Creek in the north. The purpose for the stock route was to bring cattle from the east Kimberley to the railhead at Wiluna and thence to markets in Perth. The last cattle drive was in 1958. Destroyed by the elements, the route virtually disappeared over the years and a compass was an essential requirement for the few people who travelled it; the first vehicular crossing of the entire stock route was made in 1968. Today, hundreds of people go up or down annually.

There are over 900 sand dunes to cross, the highest lying in the north. Unlike the Simpson Desert's dunes that run in parallel lines, the Canning's run in all directions, and are known as 'confused' dunes, with many of them having double or more crests that can make driving difficult. The tracks over the dunes are often rough with deep ridges.

A big feature of the Canning Stock Route is the wells. Some of them are dry, others have stagnant or brackish water, while only about nine have good water. Most of the windlasses and stock troughs are in ruins; however, Well 26 has been restored, complete with a stock trough.

Although I have a 4WD vehicle, on hearing how difficult some of the driving could be in the Great Sandy Desert, I opted to be a passenger in a 4WD escorted safari up the Canning. It was a great adventure, and I learnt more about driving 4WDs during this three-week trip than I had in the past year driving my own vehicle.

ABOVE: *Great Sandy Desert*   BELOW L: *Well 26, Canning Stock Route*   BELOW R: *Thorny Devil*

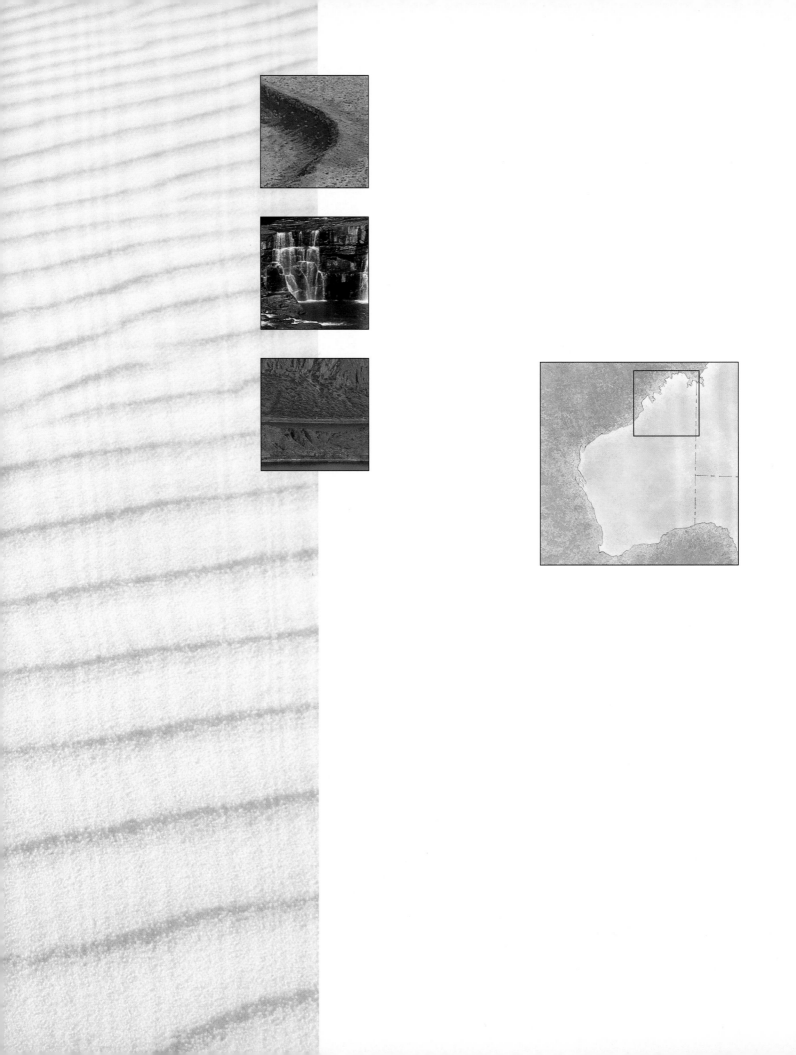

Kimberley

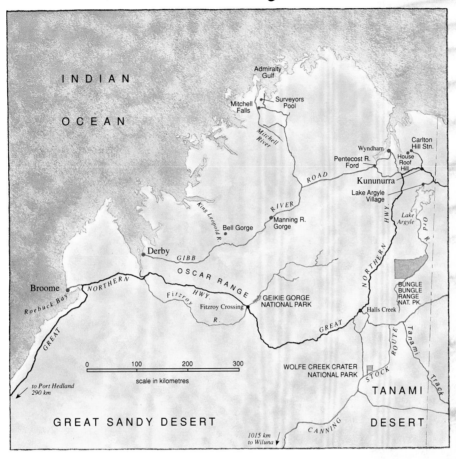

At the top end of the state is the Kimberley region, where the wet and the dry seasons are more marked, and monsoonal rains fall between December and March. Like the Pilbara, temperatures in the Kimberley are higher in the wet summer and lower in the dry winter. With the exception of coastal areas, the best months for travelling in both these regions are between May and September, the coolest time being between mid-June to the end of July. However, the Kimberley is exceptionally beautiful during the wet season.

For many people, the Kimberley is a very special region. Rich in an atmosphere different from anywhere else, its landscapes of rugged ranges, magnificent gorges, vast plains dotted with strange boab trees, and great rivers that flow for only a few months of the year, stretch the mind and evoke in the traveller a tremendous sense of awe. Somehow one has here a heightened sense of adventure, largely because this stunningly beautiful region is one of the world's great wild places.

WOLFE CREEK CRATER

The Wolfe Creek meteorite crater is the second largest in the world (the largest is in the United States). Lying at the far north-western edge of the Tanami Desert and 146 kilometres south of Halls Creek in the Kimberley, this great crater measures 850 metres in diameter and 50 metres deep. It has created worldwide scientific interest, and is regarded as the closest in appearance to the craters seen on the moon's surface. It is believed to be the largest one with the most unbroken rim—others are inclined to be very uneven. The shape of a crater is determined by the way the meteorite hits the ground: if it comes in at an angle, the crater will be more irregular than if it comes straight down, as it did at Wolfe Creek. It is not known just when the meteorite—a fragment from a 'shooting star'—hit the Earth's crust. But it escaped disintegration into dust on entering the atmosphere and landed about half a kilometre from the stream that gave the crater its name.

Since the Tanami Track has been upgraded to a reasonably good gravel road (its condition still needs to be checked before travelling), many people are now stopping to see the crater on their way to the Kimberley. I first saw it from the air, expecting it to be visually more appealing from above than from the ground. I was wrong: its perfect bowl-like shape was very impressive viewed from the top of its rim. It was easier to film from the air, however, as even my 35 mm camera's wide-angle 24 mm lens could not do justice to the sight from the rim.

A ten-minute walk from the top of the rim leads to a small group of trees growing in its centre. These trees have only appeared in recent times, and when I visited it, one of my travelling companions commented that there had been considerable growth since his last trip ten years previously. He also said that we were fortunate to be able to walk down into it: in the United States visitors must view their crater only from a specially built platform. I'm glad we are permitted to walk into Wolfe Creek Crater as it is a memorable experience.

Wolfe Creek Crater

BROOME

Most people tend to forget, as soon as they reach Broome, that any other world exists. More enthusiasm is shown for this town than any other in the entire West and, understandably, it has become a haven for thousands who migrate to this delectably warm place each winter to escape the lower temperatures of the south. It is also the gateway to the west Kimberley's wild and wonderful scenery.

Situated 2213 kilometres from Perth, Broome nestles on a finger of land that separates the wide expanse of Roebuck Bay from the Indian Ocean. Much of its tropical charm and relaxed atmosphere can be attributed to the strong oriental character it has retained from the great pearling days of last century, when many Asians came to crew the fleet of pearling luggers based here.

Today, apart from the odd one used for tourist purposes, the luggers are no longer seen moored at the town's jetty. The pearling industry began its decline soon after 1914, but the demand for cultured pearls prevented Broome from becoming a ghost town; in 1956 the first pearl farm was established, with more following in later years. These farms continue to produce the highest quality cultured pearls in the world—thanks to the Kimberley coast's clean water and its particularly rich nutrients that are brought in by the huge tides.

Broome is still the 'Port of Pearls', as the cultured pearl is very much promoted here. Even the town's annual festival is named 'Shinju Matsuri'—Festival of the Pearl. It is held for ten days every August–September at the time of a full moon so that visitors can see the magical event known as the 'Golden Staircase to the Moon'—a phenomenon that occurs only a few times a year when the full moon rises over Roebuck Bay during a low king tide. The reflection of the moonlight in pools of water left on the ocean bed creates the effect of steps.

In recent years the town has undergone many changes to cater for the fast-growing tourist industry, and at times during the winter months you would think there was a permanent Shinju festival in progress, the town is so crowded with visitors. However, despite the changes that have upset some people, Broome has retained its character, with a special atmosphere that will never entirely be lost.

Roebuck Bay, Broome

BUNGLE BUNGLE RANGE

The wild and rugged Kimberley region is ideal for concealing scenic treasures: one of its best-kept secrets over the years was the Bungle Bungle Range. Before its exposure by an aerial film crew in 1983, only the Aborigines and some pastoralists knew of its existence. So little was known about it that when the range was first publicised, one government official in Canberra faxed an associate to ask if he had heard of the Bungle Bungle. The reply fax read: 'No. Sounds like the name of a government department'.

Today it is a national park and has become a very important scenic attraction. It has significance for the local Aborigines who are involved in its management and who know it as Pernululu, while many Europeans prefer to call it 'the Bungles'. Rising from the plains as a great triangular massif, the range is cut by ravines and bound by high cliffs that in places rise to 400 metres and give way to a mass of curiously weathered orange-and-black-banded domes. It is these beehive-like formations that people come to see.

Lying 300 kilometres by road from Kununurra and about half that distance from Halls Creek, access to the range is strictly by 4WD vehicle, as the last 55 kilometres running off the highway are very rough; even worse are the tracks to Echidna Chasm and Piccaninny Creek. The two-to-three day commercial tours running from Kununurra and Halls Creek are extremely popular, and so are the aerial fixed-wing flights operating from those two towns. I believe the ultimate experience of the Bungles is a helicopter flight—with the doors off. It may seem as if the sides of the chopper are missing, but touring like this gives a heightened sense of contact with this peculiar area. These flights are so popular that a pilot and machine are stationed at the Kurrajong camp throughout the tourist season.

For photographers, the best time to fly is early morning or late afternoon. I was so enchanted with my first chopper flight that I took another the next day. It is not until you see this geological masterpiece from a close-range perspective that the full extent of the Bungles' magnificent terrain can be appreciated.

ORD RIVER

Draining a large part of the east Kimberley region, the Ord River meets the sea at Cambridge Gulf on the north coast. The rich pasturelands of the river's plains were originally settled by the Durack family who named one of their stations 'Argyle'. In the 1960s the river was dammed to trap its once-wasted colossal floodwaters and Argyle was permanently flooded; the dam wall is situated 67 kilometres upstream from Kununurra. Fed by monsoonal rains falling only in the summer wet season, the Ord fills Lake Argyle to cover approximately 740 square kilometres—or the equivalent of nine Sydney Harbours. That size will be nearly trebled when the dam fills to its maximum level, which is believed to occur about once every 150 years.

The Ord Irrigation Scheme irrigated experimental cotton crops, but pests and diseases presented too many problems; then rice was grown, but that succeeded in only feeding great flocks of birds. Today fruit, vegetables and fodder-crops are grown with some success but on a small scale. 'Kununurra is still waiting for a crop that will put it on the map', one resident said. Meanwhile, everybody enjoys the local produce, and the tourists marvel at the beauty of Lake Argyle, which nestles like a soft blue sapphire among the extraordinarily colourful Carr Boyd Ranges. Every time I see the lake from the lookout points around the dam, I feel as if I am part of a richly coloured oil painting.

Few man-made lakes are as interesting as Lake Argyle, with its rich history, the abundant wildlife, and the colourful scenery. One good way to see it and to learn something about the area is to take a boat trip from Argyle Village. On my last visit I took the half-day boat tour on the *Silver Cobbler* that went to the far end of the lake; I was curious to see the Ord where it began to look like a river again. It was an excellent trip, skippered by a local man who knew the area intimately and who showed us plenty of wildlife.

Lake Argyle aside, the Ord River has much beauty to offer elsewhere. Downstream from Kununurra there is a glorious spot: The Bush Camp. Set high on the banks of the Lower Ord at the base of House Roof Hill on Carlton Hill Station, the Bush Camp lies about 80 kilometres from the river's mouth. Here visitors can fish, explore the river, or just relax and enjoy the warm hospitality provided. I found it difficult to leave the charismatic Ord River region.

ABOVE: *Ord River, The Bush Camp*   BELOW L: *Magpie Geese*   BELOW R: *Rock Wallaby*

Lake Argyle

GEIKIE GORGE

Probably the best known gorge in the Kimberley is Geikie Gorge whose cliffs imprison the Fitzroy River for eight extremely scenic kilometres. It lies in the limestone ranges that were part of the ancient Devonian 'Great Barrier Reef', formed in a past era when part of the Kimberley was covered by tropical seas. Cut by rivers and deeply fissured by weathering, the reef is now exposed in a series of long narrow ranges that wind over the region for many kilometres and rise to heights of 100 metres between Derby and Fitzroy Crossing. The weathering continues in Geikie, as every wet season its limestone walls are washed by great floodwaters that race through the gorge.

Access is easy to Geikie Gorge National Park along a good bitumen road that leads to the carpark from Fitzroy Crossing, 20 kilometres away. Consequently the park receives many visitors—including most coaches touring the Kimberley. Camping is no longer permitted in the national park, but there are camping grounds and a motel at Fitzroy Crossing.

Between April and October the park rangers run boat-tours on the river twice daily from the carpark. The boat goes very close to the walls of the gorge that are full of great clefts, indentations and cavities marked with many colours, as if splashed with paint. In places the cliffs resemble pieces of contoured empty honeycomb; in other spots it looks as if a bricklayer has been busy. Although there is a good chance of seeing reflections on the morning tour, I prefer to tour in the afternoon because the colours are more vibrant; it is also the better tour for seeing the Johnstone's freshwater crocodiles sunning themselves on rock ledges and muddy banks. These timid reptiles usually grow to lengths of around 2.5 metres, but some may reach sizes of 4.25 metres. They have never been known to attack man.

If you miss seeing the reflections on the morning tour, and feel like taking a short walk along the western bank late in the afternoon, you may see the colourful walls mirrored in the river, as often the breezes drop just before sunset. It takes only 30 minutes over some very loose sandy sections to reach the best section of cliffs.

Geikie Gorge

GIBB RIVER ROAD

Lying in the remote country north of the Great Northern Highway in the Kimberley, the Gibb River Road is the shorter 'back track' that links Derby and Wyndham. Although it cuts off 230 kilometres for travellers who would otherwise have to go via the longer route through Halls Creek, this route is no time-saver because it is unsealed and in places very rough. However, its 646 kilometres pass through superb scenery.

Although motorists pass through a series of ranges, the two most notable are the King Leopold Range and the Cockburn Range. The King Leopold Range lies near Derby, and for about 70 kilometres the road winds through these wild rocky hills that constantly change in character and colour. The Cockburn Range, a huge plateau-topped massif with fantastic collars of pinky-brown rock, lies beside the Gibb River Road in the east; at the Pentecost River crossing, it provides a striking backdrop for the river. I love this spot at sunset, when the range becomes swathed in shades of pink and red, and in windless conditions is reflected in the water. But the river's edge is no place to linger for too long: some big saltwater crocodiles live here.

Probably the Gibb River Road is most famous for its gorges, as there are many that lie off it. My favourite used to be Manning Gorge but then I discovered Bell Gorge, a marvellous place just east of the King Leopold Range. Before 1986 few people had heard of it as it lay on private property; today the gorge is a proposed national park, and access is only for well-rewarded 4WD enthusiasts. The main pool and the gorge were larger than I had imagined, and only when I scrambled up its rocky slopes to the top of the waterfall and walked around the gorge's rim did I appreciate the full extent of the grandeur of Bell Gorge. The small pool at the top of the waterfall was particularly beautiful at sunset, when the still water reflected the clouds and surrounding range.

Officially, the Gibb River Road is not recommended for conventional vehicles or caravans, but once the wet's rains have ceased and the graders have been over the road, most 2WD vehicles can manage it if extreme care is taken. Travellers should always first check the road's condition with local authorities. Remember though, that some of the side-tracks leading to the gorges are only suitable for 4WDs.

Bell Gorge

MITCHELL PLATEAU

Until recently, few people ventured up to the Mitchell Plateau, lying inland from Admiralty Gulf on the Kimberley's north coast. Today, nearly everyone in 4WD vehicles touring the Kimberley wants to come here (the tracks on the plateau are only suitable for 4WDs). The main drawcard is the Mitchell Falls, said to be Australia's most spectacular waterfall. It is indeed during, and just after the wet season. However, by August–September the falls may be little more than a trickle—if that. From the carpark it is a hard walk to the top of the falls: the heat and rugged terrain reduce walking speed, and most people allow six hours to do the round trip.

There is more to the Mitchell Plateau than the falls. One unique feature is the livistona palms that cover large tracts of the area. I remember being quite astonished when I first saw them—I had heard there were palms on the plateau, but not *forests* of them. In places eucalypts mingle with the palms, and sometimes dominate. Apparently there used to be many more palms, in places so thick that they resembled dense green walls along the road, but in recent times fires have thinned their numbers. Some fear that if the mining company who holds the lease in the area decides to mine the extensive but low-grade bauxite deposits, there would be even fewer of these ancient palms.

It is hoped that at least a portion of the palm forests may be included in the proposed national park that will protect the Mitchell Falls, and one other notable place: Surveyors Pool.

Surveyors Pool is a deep and spacious pool surrounded by six-metre high walls of craggy white sandstone leached with colourful markings. The approach is from the cliff tops, and the easiest access to the pool is at the far end opposite the waterfall. When I was there, it was an easy enough four-kilometre walk from the carpark, but near the end the track suddenly disappeared in a sea of high cane grass and woodland. After much casting around, we eventually found it—leaving yellow markers for future walkers.

Mitchell Falls

87

BOAB TREES

A book on the West would not be complete without mentioning the boab tree, the wonderful fat-trunked, swollen-limbed tree that is a distinct feature of the Kimberley region. Confined to the far north-west of Australia, it is one of only two species in the genus, the other being found in Africa. Its botanical name is *Adansonia gregorii*, and although the tree's official common name is 'baobab', Australians find that word a mouthful and have shortened it to 'boab'.

No two trees are the same: each has its own individual character, which is best appreciated in the dry season when all leaves have dropped. Some of the young slender ones are elegant, while the old granddads look arthritic, even grotesque. Some boabs are jaunty, others are haughty, while a few are even grumpy-looking. There are lovers that fondly twist their limbs around each other, and mothers surrounded by groups of young ones. Wherever they are, these trees provide delightful entertainment for the traveller.

Boab at sunrise